ENERGY VAMPIRES

AN EMPATHS GUIDE ON HOW TO DEAL WITH
NEGATIVE PEOPLE

JENNIFER O'NEILL

Keys to the Spirit World, LLC

Kailua, HI 96734

www.keystothespiritworld.com

Formatting: Keys to the Spirit World LLC

Energy Vampires: An Empaths Guide on How to Deal With Negative People

Fourth Kindle Edition: August 2022

ISBN: 9781484068359

CHAPTER 1

WHAT IS AN ENERGY VAMPIRE?

*Y*ou've probably heard the term "energy vampires" before, especially if you're at all interested in psychic ability or psychic development. But what exactly are energy vampires? They're not real vampires. Well, I guess they're real vampires, but not like the ones you see in Twilight … "Energy vampires" feed upon your energy. In other words, their primary target is your spiritual body, not your physical body.

"Energy vampires" are people who constantly draw upon other people's energy in order to help "recharge" their own system.

What do energy vampires and negative people have in common?

They have a lower vibrational frequency. So they are looking to draw upon anyone with a higher vibrational frequency to stay charged. And this tends to have a very profound effect on your system, both spiritually and physically. Many times, they will wear you down to the point of exhaustion.

However, unless you're aware of what is happening, you may not even notice the effects these people are having in your life, on a day-to-day basis. You may just think you've had a hard day and that's why you feel so exhausted, or you may think you're just more tired than usual, but you don't know why. People don't usually think, "Maybe it's the people I'm around." In fact, for many people, this is the furthest thought from their mind. Their mind tends to relate this "drained" feeling to their job, or stress they're under at home. But think about it, what's the worst part about your job? Dealing with your boss? Dealing with impossible coworkers? Dealing with unreasonable customers? All of these stressors involve people! What about stress in your life? Many times, stress you're under in your life tends to involve friends, husband, wife, kids, parents, and people who just make you mad. More people!

So who exactly do energy vampires and negative people affect?

Simple ... Everybody!

You don't need to be a healer, energy worker, or a psychic for energy vampires and negative people to have a very profound effect on you, or on your life. Everybody is susceptible to experiencing the aftereffects of being around energy vampires and negative people. It has the same spiritual and physical side effects; some people just don't realize what's happening to them. They just think being tired is a part of life...a part of being a grown up! They think being exhausted is what everybody feels like most of time. They don't realize this isn't always how you're supposed to feel. You shouldn't feel tired most of the time. You should feel good most of the time, and tired only some of the time. If you're tired most of the time, this is a very good book for you.

CHAPTER 2

AWARENESS IS KEY!

There are certain things which you can do and be aware of when dealing with "energy vampires" in order to help minimize the effect they have on your life.

These things also tend to be the same things you would do to deal with negative people in your life, since they essentially fall into the same category, so from this point on you can use energy vampires and negative people interchangeably.

Why are some people more aware of energy vampires than others? Some of you may even be wondering, "Why have I never noticed them before, but now I do?"

People who decide they want to make a change in their life tend to become acutely aware of the negative people in their life.

Imagine it like *Star Wars*; you can feel the force of the dark side. The more you decide to enlighten yourself, become more positive, or to enhance your spirituality, this will naturally begin to raise your vibrational frequency. This shift will allow lower vibrational frequencies aka the dark side, or negativity, to become apparent on your radar. Why? Because doing all these things will help you align yourself spiritually. The more in sync become with your spiritual body, the higher your vibrational frequency rises. When this happens, lower frequencies and negativity will bother you more, and become more apparent than they ever where before. Even when your circumstances haven't changed and the same people have been in your life for many years. You've changed, you're becoming more spiritually aware and your vibration is raising.

For instance, ask yourself these things:

- Are you learning what it's like to be more positive?
- Are you learning how to change your life for the better?
- Are you on a new spiritual journey?
- Are you learning how to develop your psychic senses?
- Are you noticing more and more that negative people surround you?

Wit this new ascension energy, there is an energetic shift taking place, the vibration as a whole (universal energy, earth energy, astrological energy) is all on the rise. Which is effecting a lot of people, because they are beginning to feel their spiritual bodies awaken. Most people were only aware of their physical body before, but now this is beginning to change. They can feel this shift taking place, and people are beginning to crave spiritual growth. In attempts to help awaken and connect their spiritual and physical bodies (even though they may not be fully aware that this is happening), they embark on a new spiritual journey, figuring out how to change their lives for the better. However, one thing that begins to trip them up is they no longer know how to handle negative energy or negative people in their lives. Whereas these people never seemed to bother them so much in the past, they're having a different effect on them. It seems to bother them, it makes them a little uncomfortable.

So how do you cope with them? How do you keep them in your life and still stay positive, especially, since many times, these people are close friends and family?

This adverse reaction to negativity is new to many people. When you're not sure what to do, or how to deal with negativity, it makes this new journey harder than it has to be.

Another thing happening during this new spiritual awakening is many people are discovering they are empaths. Do you have to be an empath in order to have energy vampires or negative people affect you? No. In fact, you just have to be...well, human. But it's helpful to know if you are an empath, because empaths are way more sensitive to energy vampires and negative people than most other people. Because of this, I have devoted the next chapter empaths.

CHAPTER 3

WHAT IS AN EMPATH?

*A*s one's spiritual body begins to awaken, so does one's psychic senses. So what is an empath? An empath naturally has the ability to utilize one of the psychic senses, also known as clairsentience. People who have heightened ability in this area are referred to as empaths.

Empaths have an ability to read energy...all energy! Universal energy, emotional energy, astrological energy, spiritual energy, you name it.

However, being an empath also commonly refers to form of extrasensory perception where a person acquires psychic knowledge primarily by means of empathic feelings and emotions.

In other words, you feel the energy of what another person is projecting, emotional energy. This type of energy is created, manifested, and charged by emotions.

What's essentially happening is you can feel what is going on with another person emotionally.

Emotional energy is one of the easiest of all the universal energies to "read" or simply be aware of when you are an empath.

Even people who never thought of themselves as having any psychic ability in the past are now experiencing different things with their psychic senses. Often, however, they just don't know what's happening. Children frequently develop this ability, and they may have difficulty dealing with it. As an empath, you feel what people around you feel. When you experience other people's emotions, your mind and body can get overwhelmed and confused. You experience exactly what those around you are experiencing at that moment, regardless of the signals your mind is sending to your body. These mixed signals can leave you feeling overwhelmed and unsettled. Your mind is telling you to have a reaction to something, but you're not sure what you're reacting to. This can also occur when you think of something or someone.

When this happens, *when your physical body and its emotions are reacting on their own, without being triggered*, your mind then searches for a reason. You assume it's you, when it's not you at all.

Empathy is most commonly experienced when another person is right in front of you. It's not a problem if the person right in front of you is generally a positive, uplifting person. If this is the case, then it can be rather enjoyable. However, when you're dealing with energy vampires or negative people, it's not so enjoyable! You may begin to feel all kinds of negative emotions, and this psychic sense can immediately become overwhelmed, even when you do not know them.

For instance, if someone has had a very bad day, they may act cheerful, but in their presence, you can feel their true emotions. You may feel upset or sad for no discernible reason. Your mind and body aren't on the same page. Since you had a good day, there is no rhyme or reason for you to feel bad. When this person walks away, however, you feel normal again. As an empath, your body will mimic the true emotions of another person when you think of them, or when you're in their presence.

Now think about this for a minute. If you're an empath, and your body mimics other people's emotions and the way they're feeling inside, what kind of effect do you think it will have on your system when negative people surround you? Just think of the impact! They're not even your own emotions, but it feels as if they are. So how does that make it better? It doesn't. That's why it's so important for you to understand if you're an empath, and if you are, what you can do to avoid feeling like this all the time.

This may be a good time, whether you are an empath or not, to take a mental inventory of all of the people who you come into contact with on a daily basis, or the people who you most surround yourself with. Such as:

- Friends
- Family
- Coworkers
- Acquaintances

If you wish you can write these people down on a piece of paper. Include them even if you just talk to them on the phone—this is also considered contact. You don't have to be physically in their presence every day to have them on this list. The next thing you want to do is determine if these people are mostly positive, or mostly negative. Then, determine how you feel when you're around them. Do you feel happy, sad, anxious, stressed, and tense, or relaxed, happy, and wonderful? Notice what type of effect their presence, or

contact, has on your system. This is the first step to awareness. You'll learn how to deal with them later in this book.

Children are often empaths. This is really important to
know, especially if you have children or grandchildren in
your life. As a child, you were most likely very affected by
other people's emotions. Often, children grow out of being
an empath during their teenage years, as they learn to "put a
cork" on their psychic senses. Parents often don't realize
their own children are very connected and empathetic to
their feelings. So if the parent is consistently angry or upset,
even when trying to hide it, your children most likely can
"feel" right through your cover.

CHAPTER 4

SIX SIGNS YOU ARE AN EMPATH

So how do you know if you're an empath? In this chapter I've put together a list of six signs which are very good indicators that you are an empath. You don't have to have all six signs in order to be an empath, you may only have two or three of them. But you'll know right away after reading through this list, if you are, or if you aren't.

1) Do you feel "overwhelmed" when going to a place filled with a lot of people?

Do you feel overwhelmed when going into a mall, a sporting event, or Wal-Mart? Somewhere where there might be a lot of people? Do you find yourself wanting to go, but when you get there you feel anxious, unsettled, or "very off" and you don't know why? It doesn't always have to be a public place. It could be to someone's house party, a baby shower, a wedding, or Thanksgiving dinner; anywhere where you are around a lot of people. It's not uncommon for an empath to have an anxiety disorder. Why does this happen? Because empaths pick up on a flood of emotions from everybody all at once. You're like a radio, picking up all kinds of "emotional" signals from everywhere. As an empath, you have the tendency to tune into everything and everyone unless you train yourself otherwise. And if you don't know what's happening, your spiritual and physical bodies become overwhelmed trying to make sense of it all. Your spiritual body is receiving information, and your physical body is trying to process it all, but it's making no sense in your mind. Your own emotional state doesn't match how your body is reacting physically, hence that "overwhelming" feeling.

2) Can you always tell when someone is lying to you?

Have you always been able to tell when someone is telling the truth, or lying to you? Even if they do it flawlessly, it's something you just "know," or can "feel" and sense. Or can you feel if someone is being deceptive, even when you have no reason not to believe them? As an empath, it's very easy to tell if someone is telling the truth or lying to you, because when someone is lying to you, they generally have an anxious feeling, their heart rate is higher, and they almost feel a bit flighty to you. There is also a feeling of insincerity that accompanies the lie. These types of emotions are easily transferred and "readable" to an empath. They come across very clear, as you will really be able to tell they're not your own emotions at the time. When you feel this deception or insincerity, your mind immediately shifts to whoever is in your presence. You'll usually know the answer to this question right away.

3) Do you have random emotions or mood swings, especially when in someone else's presence, or when you think about them, which makes no sense to you?

Do you ever have random emotions or mood swings, which don't follow a thought?

In some instances you may find you're not thinking of anything in particular, yet your body is reacting emotionally. If your emotions don't seem to be following a thought which coincides with that particular emotion, you're most likely picking up on someone else's feelings, feelings that aren't your own. Remember, when you think of something or someone, that thought is then coupled with your perception and it causes you to have an emotional reaction or physical response. Your mind and its thoughts trigger your physical body and your emotions, causing a reaction. When this doesn't happen, say your physical body and your emotions are reacting on their own, without being triggered. If this happens when in someone else's presence, it's a very good indicator they are not your feelings at all. It indicates you are picking up on someone else's feelings like a radio, a sign of being an empath.

4) Can you feel someone else's physical ailments?

Do you ever feel sick, or experience a pain, which makes no sense to you at all, only to find out later that it coincided with a symptom a friend or family member was experiencing? Maybe you were feeling nauseous and found out later someone close to you had the flu, or you had a stomach cramp and found out they had appendicitis.

For instance, my daughter has a very good dental history. She has never had cavities in her permanent teeth, only as a child. All of her permanent teeth have been sealed and she has good dental hygiene habits. Despite all of her good habits, recently, she began experiencing some tooth pain. We couldn't see anything on her tooth which would indicate a cavity; in fact, her teeth looked very good. Yet the pain was very real to her. This pain went on for about two or three weeks, when it began to bother her so much she decided maybe she better make a dentist appointment. She thought maybe there was something going on we couldn't see. Later that day, her father went into the dentist to get a cavity filled on a tooth that had started bothering him a few weeks prior. The next day, after my husband's cavity had been filled, my daughter's mysterious tooth pain had disappeared! She no longer experiences any tooth pain.

Mysterious pains or physical ailments which "disappear" are also a good indicator. This is not as common as the other signs, so if it hasn't happened to you, don't give it too much thought.

5) Do you instinctively know what someone needs to feel better emotionally or physically?

Can you predict or instinctively know what someone else needs to feel better, even when they don't quite know what they need themselves? Do you know what someone is thinking or trying to say, especially when they're not expressing themselves clearly?

This is why empaths often become healers, energy workers, and psychics. They have the ability to instinctively "know" what patients and clients need. When I say healers, this also refers to people such as doctors and psychologists—anyone who is has an instinctive gift of knowing how to help heal people. There are many types of healers out in the world who come from all walks of life.

You don't need to be a healer, however; you may just be that person or friend who everyone is "drawn" to for advice. Are you the go to person in your group of friends or family who everyone goes to when they have problems? Do you seem to give out a lot of advice (because they ask, not because they need it) to the people around you? Do people always tell you they feel much better after talking with you? These are good indicators of being an empath.

6) Do you feel emotionally of physically drained after being around an individual, or a group of people, to the point of needing to take a nap, or physically not feeling well?

When you are around an individual or a group of people, do you ever find yourself feeling any of these things afterwards:

- Shaky
- Achy
- Light headed
- Weak
- Nauseous
- Anxious
- Out of Body
- Low blood sugar feeling (when full)

These feelings are not experienced prior to, but only after having been around an individual or a group of people, then, it usually takes a couple of hours to feel "normal" again. Or do you ever find yourself so completely exhausted that all you want to do is take a nap when you get home? You feel like your body and mind are completely void of energy. So you lay down, hoping to recover from this lethargic feeling which has taken over your entire being. After a few hours, you can finally start to feel your energy return again. If you experience three or more of these things after being around a certain individual or a group of people consistently, it's a pretty good indicator you're an empath.

It's not uncommon for empaths to overeat. Many times they don't realize they feel this way from being drained of so much energy, instead their mind attributes these feelings to how it feels when the physical body needs fuel. Naturally, they do what they think will help—they eat. What they don't realize is this is also the way the spiritual body feels when it needs fuel or energy.

These are six clear indicators of being an empath. If you are an empath, there will be no doubt in your mind after reading these signs. You won't be thinking, "I could be, I have some of them, but I am not sure," or "Well ... I've experienced that before." You'll have an "aha" moment of "It all makes sense now!" It's something you will know immediately to the core of your being.

*NOTE: I've created a quiz for those who are still on the fence and wondering if they are an empath. Link available here: www.keystothespiritworld.com

Want to Find Out if You
Have a Heightened
Ability to Read Energy?
Find Out Now!

Empath Quiz

CHAPTER 5

I AM AN EMPATH! NOW WHAT?

*B*y this time you should've had your "aha" moment and know whether or not you're an empath. If you are, and you didn't know it before, don't panic and lock yourself inside the house just yet. Yes, being an empath is one of the most difficult psychic senses to have. However, it's only difficult if:

You are unaware you are an empath. (Problem solved already by the "aha" moment).

You have no idea how to protect yourself. (Problem solved by reading this book).

So, like all things, it doesn't have to be difficult, it can become easily manageable. Mostly by one simple thing…

Awareness.

When you finally realize you're an empath, you can finally begin to differentiate your own feelings from everyone else's.

*Just by simply being aware you are an empath, your mind can
more easily detect your feelings from someone else's.*

In fact, just being aware will change everything for you. It
will allow you to make the separation between their feelings
and yours. Your mind and body will no longer enter situa-
tions only to feel "blindsided" by a powerful wave of
emotions; you'll become more prepared for it.

Think of it like this. Imagine you were suddenly hit by a
hurricane out of nowhere. You had no warning, and since
you were completely unaware, you had taken no precautions,
such as boarding up windows, preparing for high winds and
rain, making sure you had proper supplies such as candles,
food, and propane for cooking. So when the hurricane hits,
you panic. Windows are broken, rain is coming in everywhere, and your electricity goes out. After hours of enduring
this endless storm, you are left with the aftermath. You go
days with no power, cleaning up the mess, and struggling
with the food and water situation. Eventually you recover
just fine. But you didn't weather the storm like you could
have, and you're a little bit traumatized from the experience.
Now imagine a different scenario in which you were more
aware of what was about to happen. Let's say you were faced
with the same hurricane, only you knew it was coming.
You're aware of the things you need to do to in order to
prepare for the storm. You board up windows and secure
your things. You make sure you have plenty of food, water,
and supplies to last a week or two in case of a power outage.
The storm hits and you know it will be several hours before it
passes, so you occupy your time. Windows aren't broken, and
rain does not enter as you have done a good job preparing.
When the storm passes, you have no power, but everything is
intact. You don't have any major damage and have plenty of

supplies to hold you over until things get restored. Now which scenario feels better to you? See how you can be in the same situation, yet have very different experiences?

This is similar to what happens to you when you're an empath. You can go into a situation completely unaware and unprepared. Or you can go into a situation where you can weather the same storm, only to come out of it relatively good, and not traumatized. You can prepare yourself.

Three Things Every Empath Should Do:

1) Bubble Yourself

Actually, all people should do this, as it is a protection barrier. It helps to keep your energy in and keeps unwanted energy from sticking to you. It also shields you from having your energy and system drained by energy vampires and negative people.

This is just like it sounds. Before you go into a place filled with people you need to bubble yourself. This is like a quick meditation but it doesn't have to take long. You can easily do this in a couple of minutes, but it's important that you do it. A quick two-minute bubble is way better than no bubble at all! In fact, that's all you really need. I'll walk you through the steps here.

Find a quiet place where you won't be disturbed. However, if you forget to do this before you go out, you can do this in the car before you go in someplace easily enough.

Sit comfortably in an upright position. Hands to your side and feet flat on the floor, don't cross your hands, feet or legs.

Close your eyes and concentrate on your breathing. Slow your breathing to a relaxed state.

When your breathing is rhythmic, concentrate on relaxing all of the muscles in your body.

Next, imagine a white light of pure powerful energy coming down from above your head, this white light is from the Holy Spirit, God, or source (whatever you are comfortable with). Feel this energy come through the roof of your house or car, and allow it to gently enter your system through your seventh chakra (the top of your head). This energy feels good, empowering and protective.

Allow this white light energy to touch each chakra while it recharges your spiritual body. Continue to let the white light flow through your system until you feel fully charged.

Next allow the excess energy to fill a bubble around you. "Feel and direct" this white light energy by way of thought to form a large bubble surrounding your entire being. This powerful white light is recharging your energetic field with new energy, strong and protective energy. Feel this energy charging your system as it continues out into the bubble. Once the bubble is full, feel the strength of the bubble. Nothing can penetrate the bubble from the outside. It's like a protective barrier around your being.

Remain in this state until you feel a sense of completion, then release this image into the Universe and go about your day.

There is no right or wrong amount of time you spend creating the bubble, you should adjust the time to whatever feels right to you. This bubble will protect you against other people's energy and energy vampires, who are unknowingly trying to draw energy from you. It will also help to protect you from a flood of emotions coming at you all at once when you're around a large group of people. It's harder for you to pick up their "radio signal" as the bubble dissipates it. These things are what leave you feeling shaky, weird, light headed, etc.

2) A Quick Mind/Body Check

When you're around someone or a group of people and you begin to feel "not right" or emotional, do a quick mind/body check by asking yourself these questions.

Did I have a thought that coincides with these feelings?

Did something happen earlier in the day that these feelings make sense with?

If the answer to both questions are no, then make the separation. Understand that these feelings are coming from someone else (and it may not be from the person in front of you at the time, so don't spend too much time trying to figure out who it is coming from), then release these feelings. *By release them, I mean do not own them!* When you make a mental note to release these emotions, they will pass through your system. In other words, they won't hang out and "park" themselves there. It may take a minute or two, and sometimes even hours, but they will go, and the impact on your system will be minimal. If you own these emotions and feelings, they will park themselves in your system, causing you physical discomfort, sometimes turning into physical distress if allowed to. Allow them to move on, and note that you will feel better soon.

3) Exercise

I'm not just saying this to keep you healthy, so don't roll your eyes yet. Exercise is very important when you are an empath. It helps to:

Keep your spiritual and physical bodies in harmony.

When you keep your spiritual and physical bodies in harmony, it will strengthen your energetic system, which is very powerful. It will also allow you to have more control over the energies flowing in and out of your bodies.

Ground your system. (Which is so important it will also have its own chapter.)

Exercise grounds your system, which releases excess energy and allows it to dissipate into the earth very quickly; much faster than if you are just sitting around. As an empath, you are picking up excess stuff every day, from everywhere. So it's very important not to let this excess energy clutter your energetic system, and in order to keep your system clean, you must rid yourself of it.

If you have just realized you are an empath, the things in this chapter will help to change things dramatically for you. You'll feel like a whole new person. I strongly suggest you do all of these things on a daily basis for a while, then you can go to an as needed basis.

CHAPTER 6

HOW TO SPOT AN "ENERGY VAMPIRE"

So how do you spot an energy vampire? Since I've given you such great news up until this point I'm sure you want to steer clear of all of them. However, you most likely won't be able to do that, and you may not even want to. What you can do is become more aware of who they are, and that will minimize the effect they have on your system, because there are things you can do to counter act their "energy draining abilities."

There are a few very easy ways to tell if someone is an energy vampire, and some that are not so easy. For the most part, however, they do not try to disguise themselves in any way, because they do not feel anything is wrong with them. They feel normal.

Five Signs Of An "Energy Vampire"

1) Negative people!

Negative people are very easily spotted, especially since they tend to pride themselves on the fact they think this way.

They are negative thinkers and complain about everything. They are very powerful in their negative thinking, even sometimes to the point of being overbearing.

- They like to point out in a very arrogant manner how stupid people are around them, people who believe in a better way, or believe that things will get better.

- They don't understand why these people refuse to accept the fact life sucks, and bad things happen.

- They complain about everything, from the weather, to what is on (or not on) TV.

- They're argumentative about everything. If you say the sky is blue, they will say it is aqua, or that it is actually an illusion.

Negative people *love* to bring people down to their level, or bring other people's vibration down. Just like negative people become very apparent on your radar when you begin to raise your vibration. Positive people are very much on the radar of negative people, so if you're positive or becoming enlightened, or more spiritual, you'll stand out to them, making them uncomfortable. Since they're also very aware of any mismatched vibrations, they pride themselves on being able to bring other people down to their level (or vibration). This may not be something they say verbally, but internally this is something they seek and strive for. It makes them feel more comfortable.

2) People who are depressed, sad, needy, or critical most of the time.

This is similar to number one, however, instead of being overbearing, they have more of a victim undertone. Everyone has felt this way on occasion, and experiencing these emotions from time to time is completely normal. However, what I'm talking about are people who chronically feel this way, with only brief bouts of happiness. These people are not hard to spot; in fact, you probably can name all of the people you know like this in under a minute.

- They are depressed, and sad, with a victim-like undertone to who they are.

- They seem to be a victim to everything.

- They may have an "I'm not good enough or smart enough" attitude.

- They take no responsibility for their own life or situation, because it's not their fault, life has dealt them a bad hand.

- They are very NEEDY people.

Now granted some of these people do need to be on medication, or need professional help. But others do not. They're just cranky, needy people! They don't think there's anything wrong with them, and make this behavior a lifestyle.

These types of people will most likely never change, even when you sit down and try and help them find a way out. You must always be there holding their hand, telling them things will be okay, guiding them towards the right direction.

They're incredibly draining and frustrating to deal with because they're also very deceiving.

You can spend a great amount of time helping them with a situation, or helping them to "feel better," and you can actually begin to feel like you're making some progress. They appear to be a little bit better, and express eternal gratitude for you having helped them. So you leave, feeling like you did a really good deed for the day, only to realize later it was a temporary "feel better" moment. When you weren't around, they went right back to square one. So you start over again, trying to guide them towards a better life. You can clearly see it, why can't they?

Because, this is who they are, a better life is unreachable.

You can't, and won't ever be able to help someone in this situation. If this is a repetitive pattern, they need a professional who is not emotionally invested in the outcome, and most likely this is not you. They need to find it within themselves to want to make a change in their life and you can't do it for them, it has to be an internal wish.

These types of people tend to be very comfortable where they're at in life; we're just uncomfortable watching them stay there.

This is no joke. People may resist moving out of their comfort zone with all of their might; this is a comfort zone for some people. They need their own "aha" moment, and unfortunately, this is something which has to be discovered on their own.

3) People who are searching to fill a void in their life.

This can be a tricky one, because unlike the other four signs here, this one isn't always easily detected. When people are unfulfilled in their own life, sometimes it's very easy to tell, as they will represent some of the other signs as well. But sometimes, when people begin to search for another way of thinking, or they begin to search for a purpose, which fulfills them, they can become what is called a "human sponge," which is both good and bad. They will sponge up knowledge, and they crave it, as if they have been in the desert without water for a very long time. The knowledge begins to feel like replenishment to their system, just as the water would. However, human sponges also tend to soak up as much energy as they can from the outside world, which often will include you and your energy, if you're in their vicinity.

These people are usually very nice, well-meaning people, in search of something better for themselves.

This is why it can be so tricky; they aren't negative, depressed, sad, or even critical, but they're just lost souls trying to figure things out. In fact, from the outside looking in, they can frequently seem very pleasant, but with a newfound thirst for knowledge also comes a newfound thirst for energy, which results in becoming an energy vampire. As these people begin to find their way, and find purpose in their life, their sponge will begin to fill up. They will no longer need to be an energy vampire as they begin to replenish and recharge their own system.

4) Drama queens.

This is pretty self explanatory, but in case you don't know what a drama queen is, they tend to like drama, or be very drawn to it. They like to cause trouble and get everyone fighting. This can become a very addicting type of behavior, because drama queens like the way it feels when energy is all stirred up in a chaotic manner. It gives them excitement! What's really happening, however, is this type of person needs to have drama going on to distract themselves from feeling unfulfilled in their own life. So they cause a distraction … aka drama.

When you're doing something exciting, rewarding, or fulfilling with your life, you can feel the energy stirring internally. Positive stirring of energy feels good ... it feels exciting! When you're unfulfilled on a soul level, however, you don't feel any energy stirring up inside. Sometimes people try and figure out how to mimic that feeling. These people will frequently mistake chaotic energy for the positive, fulfilling energy you feel stirring inside when you're doing something rewarding.

5) Angry people.

This can be a rough one. Angry people, like some of the other "energy vampires," are also very easy to spot. However, these energy vampires are different.

These people can be very, very intense.

When dealing with angry people, they draw energy from you in a totally different manner. You put your guard up ... literally! You put up an energetic shield in order to protect yourself. This energetic shield is a real thing. When you feel as if you're walking on eggshells and feel like you need to have your guard up, your spiritual body will put up an energetic guard or shield.

An energetic shield will protect your spiritual self from their intense anger and energy.

You will expend a lot of energy creating this shield out of necessity and protection. Angry people will then draw upon the energy used to create this shield. They will also go on attack. Here are some ways in which angry people may try and attack you:

- Verbally.
- Physically.
- Talk about you behind your back.
- Sabotage you when they can.
- Do what they can to make your life miserable.

These people tend to have a vicious and evil undertone to them. Their intentions aren't good, and they seek out people to destroy emotionally or otherwise. This is "the dark side." When you have to protect yourself energetically, verbally, or physically from someone consistently, there's no way to deal with this type of situation other than cutting them out of your life ... period!

Are you an energy vampire?

Those are some easy ways to spot energy vampires. So how do you tell if you're one?

Well, it's pretty safe to say you have most likely been one on more than one occasion during your lifetime.

In fact, I have yet to run into someone who hasn't been an energy vampire at least once. However, that being said, most "balanced" people won't stay this way for very long; they'll usually snap out of this state very quickly. In other words, it will only be for temporary, and that's okay. We're all human and we experience different things throughout our lifetime. The important thing is how we handle the difficult times and that we allow ourselves to let go and move forward. So don't be too judgmental of energy vampires, for some people it may be temporary. Just be aware of them and learn how to protect yourself, as many people are dedicated to making it a lifestyle!

CHAPTER 7

EFFECTS "ENERGY VAMPIRES" HAVE ON YOUR SPIRITUAL BODY

What is the spiritual body? Your spiritual body is similar to your physical body only in energy form (see diagram below). It contains your Soul DNA or spiritual genetic system and the essence of who you are. It is "you" in your natural state.

Your spiritual body brings your physical body to life.

Without your spiritual body, it's not possible for you to exist in the physical world. When you're born, your spiritual body enters the physical realm and connects itself to your physical body through energy centers. These energy centers are what people refer to as your Chakras or Chakra System. When the two bodies merge together, your physical body is given "life." Your physical body would be "lifeless" without your spiritual body. I'm sure many of you have experienced this lifeless feeling when you have been around a loved one who has passed, or who has left this physical plane. You can no longer feel them. It's weird to many, especially since your loved one visually looks the same, however, they don't feel the same. Your spiritual body is the power, which allows your physical body function or operate.

The Seven Chakras

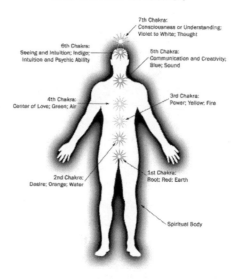

7th Chakra:
Consciousness or Understanding;
Violet to White; Thought

6th Chakra:
Seeing and Intuition; Indigo;
Intuition and Psychic Ability

5th Chakra:
Communication and Creativity;
Blue; Sound

4th Chakra:
Center of Love; Green; Air

3rd Chakra:
Power; Yellow; Fire

2nd Chakra;
Desire; Orange; Water

1st Chakra:
Root; Red; Earth

Spiritual Body

To understand what I mean, here's a quick lesson on the spiritual body. Your spiritual body is made primarily of energy, and just like many things which produce energy and hold a charge, your spiritual body needs to replenish itself, and in essence recharge itself on a daily basis. Imagine that your spiritual body is similar to a rechargeable battery, in the sense that it can acquire, store, and expend energy. Your spiritual body will hold a charge for a while, but how long you can hold the charge depends on the battery (each individual), which is determined by your vibration. Various ways in which you use your battery will also determine how fast you will drain the energy which you have stored, resulting in the need to be recharged again.

Three Most Common Ways to Expend or Use Energy:

- Trying to help or "fix" other people, or their problems.

- Burning mental energy when trying to deal with someone, or a situation.

- Going against the natural flow of the universe, or trying to force a different outcome.

These three things are exhausting. Our spiritual bodies can, and many times will, use up a lot of energy on a daily basis depending on how we *choose* to use it.

More importantly, this can also be determined by who we surround ourselves with. Other people can and will drain energy from your system in the attempt to recharge their own system.

To be fair, most energy vampires will do this unknowingly. They don't know how to necessarily draw other people's energy from them for their own benefit, rather they're just *drawn* to people who make them feel:

- Good
- Happy
- Positive
- Uplifted
- Or just better

Part of the reason energy vampires feel so good when they're around these people who they're drawn to is because they are essentially being recharged by the other person; in other words, they're stealing energy away from them. If you are that other person, however, it leaves you feeling drained and wanting to take a nap, since a lot of your energy has just been high jacked!

Energy vampires are not always strangers; in fact, many times they're close friends and family members. Unfortunately 70% of the population tends to offer and hold a lower vibration. So if you're one of the 30% who tend to hold a higher vibration more often than not, you're most likely surrounded by energy vampires purely through statistics. It can be really, really difficult when you're one of the 30% and you're around someone who holds a low vibration.

It actually can make you feel physically uncomfortable.

Why?

Because when your vibration is low you don't reproduce the same amount energetically as when your vibration is high. When your vibration is high, you constantly replenish yourself, when your vibration is low, this doesn't happen; you have what is called an energy leakage. In other words, you won't hold a charge for very long.

If you can't hold a charge, you'll be in constant need of replenishment.

People who hold a low vibration will drain their battery three to four times faster than people who hold a higher vibration.

When you hold a higher vibration, you can essentially become a target for energy vampires without even knowing it. How do you become a target?

Happy people offer a high vibration, and when happy people are around people who aren't so happy (low vibration), you have mismatched vibrations, and both vibrations will become magnified.

Your vibration (whether it is high or low) will become very noticeable, internally. It doesn't matter if you're the unhappy or sad one, it will have this kind of effect. If your vibration is higher than the other person, it will become very noticeable to you. If your vibration is lower than the other person, it will also become very apparent. When you're the unhappy one, many times your first reaction is to make this magnified unhappy feeling, or low vibration (which has now become undeniably the focus of your attention), to stop. You just want this feeling to go away, you don't want to be so aware of it. It doesn't feel good! The fastest way to make this feeling go away is to bring the other person's vibration down to your level. *Bring it down so you're a closer vibrational match.* The closer your vibration is to another person, the less you notice the mismatched vibrations, and the better you feel, so problem solved!

They will say negative things to you; anything that makes you feel bad, so your vibration is lowered.

CHAPTER 8

EFFECTS "ENERGY VAMPIRES" HAVE ON
YOUR PHYSICAL BODY

*N*ot only do energy vampires affect your spiritual body, but they affect your physical body as well. And like all physical symptoms or side effects, people tend to pay more attention to these things when they seem more real or urgent.

These things can last anywhere from minutes to hours. You may experience them while in the presence of energy vampires, or shortly thereafter. While anyone is susceptible to experiencing these things, again, they are particularly common for empaths to experience, as they are VERY susceptible to energy vampires. You read about these things in the empath chapter, but now you will learn about what takes place and causes these things to happen.

1) You may feel like you need to take a nap.

You may find that you just feel completely exhausted. So much so, that all you want to do is to take a nap. Why? Because when you've been depleted of energy from an energy vampire, the fastest and most natural way to recharge your system is to spiritually align yourself again. How do you spiritually align yourself? Through sleep or meditation. When you sleep or meditate, it's like plugging yourself back into an energy or power source for your spiritual body. You're no longer resisting, but allowing yourself to come into contact with your spirit's natural energy source, which will offer a charge to your system, just like you would plug in your laptop into a wall outlet to recharge the battery.

2) You may find you feel physically drained, sometimes, to the point of feeling physically ill.

Why does this happen?

When you allow yourself to be completely depleted of energy, it can affect your physical body to the point of not feeling well.

You may feel nauseous, or have an upset tummy, body aches, and sometimes you can even feel like you're going to throw up. This is what you feel like when your spiritual body becomes too low on the energy it needs to sustain itself. These things can vary for everyone. For instance, if I do an event where I'm doing around ten hours of psychic readings, I begin to feel achy all over, especially my joints. I also feel depleted in some other ways as well, but the achy thing bothers me the most. My energy is much stronger now than it was when I was younger. When I was younger, if I did readings for two to three hours, I would often feel shaky and nauseous, depending on the group I was reading for. Only once in my life have I felt like I was going to throw up; it was when I was in the presence of someone in particular. Most of the time you can take precautions and do some of the tricks you will learn here before this happens, and it will work out just fine. You'll be able to minimize the effect energy vampires will have in your life. I'm a very strong empath, however, and I had a family member I had to eventually cut ties with. She was a very powerful energy vampire and after about ten years of trying to figure out the best way to deal with her, I came to the conclusion that cutting her out of my life was the only way to do it. It got to the point where I couldn't deal with her at all. The phone would ring, I would see it was her, and my stomach would immediately become upset. If I talked with her, I would often feel ill to the point of throwing up. The worst thing about these types of energy vampires is their persistence. They continuously try and contact you. When my children got old enough to get upset when she called (they were also empaths and didn't like her energy at all!) That's when I drew the line. No more contact. It's not always easy, but it was the best thing to do for my family and me.

This only happens in extreme instances, but it's not uncommon. You can't predict running into strangers who might make you feel this way (although this is exactly what the bubble exercise is for), however, if you find anyone in your life such as friends or family members who leave you feeling this way, it might be best to completely cut them out of your life for the time being, or until circumstances change.

3) You may find yourself feeling very anxious or shaky during and/or after being in the presence of a particular person, or a group of people.

Energy drainage can also leave you feeling anxious or shaky. This can occur when you are around one person or a group of people. You can usually tell when it's from energy depletion because prior to being around these particular people, you usually feel fine. It's not uncommon for people who are consistently drained of energy from exposure to energy vampires to be diagnosed with an anxiety disorder.

They can't figure out what's causing the anxiety, which leaves them feeling even more anxious and confused. Energy depletion can also cause you to feel shaky and weak, similar to what happens when you experience low blood sugar, only at the time you're full. But the feeling is the same; shaky, weak, lethargic, and drained, so eating seems to calm some people, even when they know they're not hungry. This is why some empaths can tend to overeat, causing weight issues.

CHAPTER 9

EIGHT TIPS FOR DEALING WITH "ENERGY VAMPIRES" & NEGATIVE PEOPLE

*S*o now that you're aware of what an energy vampire is, how to spot them, and probably have a good idea of who they are in your life, now what? What do you do when you're in their presence? Here are eight simple tips for dealing with energy vampires and negative people.

1) Awareness!

Awareness is always the key when you're dealing with psychic senses. When you're aware of what energy vampires are, then it's good idea to take a mental note of all of the people in your life who fit this description so you know who they are. They may be people who you are around often, friends, family, and coworkers. Don't freak out if this list contains most of the people you know, like I mentioned, it's likely that 70% of the people you know will match this description. But when you are aware of who they are, you can prepare yourself before being in their presence.

2) Bubble yourself.

This is the short meditation which you learned in the empath chapter. I actually suggest that upon becoming aware of energy vampires, you bubble yourself every morning after you wake up. Then bubble yourself again before going "into the line of fire," so to speak, or before you go into a place in which you feel you might be vulnerable. This may be a place filled with a lot of people, or somewhere you might come into contact with people who are anxious, stressed out, or unhappy.

3) Learn how to not take things personally.

This will help you to strengthen your energy.

When someone says something to upset you, or says something mean to you, it's hard not to take things personally. It's hard not to get your feelings hurt, or not to become upset, because it feels like you've just been assaulted somehow. This is a very common reaction, yet it's not the best reaction to have. When you take things personally your energy shifts; you shift into a victim mentality. Victims are very prone to energy leaks and your system will feel weak, not strong. Plus, it's important to remember:

When someone says something intentionally to hurt you (even if they are good people), it's done with the intent of bringing your vibration down.

It doesn't make what they said true, or even valid, but it makes their intention clear, to hurt you. When you understand that even good people make bad choices sometimes, and do not own what they say to you, because it's not your stuff, it's their stuff, it can be much more easily disregarded with minimal hurt. (This isn't always easy, but it gets easier as you become more aware of other people's intentions, and why they behave this way). If you continue to take things personally, you make yourself an easy target for a lot of people. I don't mean to become cold hearted and emotionless, but only to take what other people say and use it to help shift your perspective. Use their words as an indicator of the emotional place they're in, right at the moment, and then ask yourself, "What's causing them to want to bring my vibration down?" When you look at them and try to figure that out, the mean thing they said to you won't stick to your heart, it will bounce off, allowing you to release it right away, as you're preoccupied with trying to figure out the answer to this question. And you will discover, most of the time, you know the answer to this question right away!

4) Find a subject they like to talk about.

When people find a subject or something they like to talk about, you'll feel their energy shift right away. Their vibration immediately begins to rise. It's one of the best tricks I've ever learned. When you find yourself around someone who is negative, find their soft spot, and ask them about it.

It's all about distraction and redirecting their energy towards something that brings them joy.

Happiness and joy will always raise your vibration, no matter who you are. They'll forget about everything else for a minute, and they'll get excited. For instance, if you know they love to garden, talk to them about gardening. If they like sports, ask them what's new with their favorite sports team. You don't have to know a single thing about the subject they're interested in, just ask them questions. People love to answer questions in an area of interest to them. It makes them feel good, and you may even learn something during this process.

5) Limit your time with them.

If they call you on the phone, don't always answer, and when you do, keep it short. If you see them in person, excuse yourself quickly, even if you have to make up something to do. Yes, even if you have to lie! I know, but many times it's the only way to politely excuse yourself, especially if you don't want to hurt their feelings. Most people feel they must deal with their family members no matter what, just because they are family. Not true. It's a choice to spend time with them, whether it's by phone or in person. And if family members are causing you discomfort, you're allowed to limit your time with them. It doesn't make you a bad person; it makes you and your family members different people with very different vibrations. It's important to stay spiritually and physically healthy. This doesn't make you selfish, it makes you smart.

Steer clear of people who often use the words "you're selfish." It's a HUGE indicator of being an energy vampire and of low vibration!

These are *the worst* people to be around! What these people are really saying is, "You're not doing what makes me feel good! You're only doing what makes you feel good and that's selfish!" What? Isn't that what we're supposed to do? Guide ourselves towards happiness … always? Raise our vibration? Find internal happiness? You're not responsible for anyone else's happiness, yet often, other people will try and hold you responsible for theirs. The funny thing is, ALL these people really care about is how they feel and the kicker is you have no control over how they feel, it's all controlled by their own perception! You can care about how other people feel, and understand that many times, what you do will only change how they feel temporarily. In fact, it really has no effect on their happiness at all; it only causes them to have a temporary shift in their perspective. So it's best to make good choices for yourself in the meantime.

6) Don't try to fix other people.

And for God's sake ... don't get sucked into their vibrational universe! Many times when you begin to find your own way in life, and you begin to raise your own vibration, it can be hard not to want to help others around you. Because it feels good, you want everyone to experience what you are feeling, especially the people you love. When you begin to raise your vibration, those same people will frequently begin to come to you for advice and guidance, wanting to learn what you know, and do what you're doing. If they are of high vibration it's great, because you will see them learn and grow right away. They'll take information you share with them and run with it immediately! Other times, when they're committed to their low vibration as a lifestyle, those people will never change. They take the information and the help, yet they tend to stay in the exact same place, needing more information and more help. And when dealing with these types of people, the indicators are very clear you won't see any progress. They're hard to help, because they'll try and suck you into their world, the world of low vibration. Yes ... they can and will actually lower your vibration if you're not careful! Just by spending too much time with people of low vibration, it can actually shift and lower your own vibration. If you begin to feel this happening, save yourself ... and don't get sucked in!

7) Make good choices on who you surround yourself with.

Pay close attention to the people you currently surround yourself with. The people you talk with most often on the phone, the people you spend the most time with in person, and the people you are consistently around during other times, such as at work.

Vibrations, whether they are low or high, will attract other like (or similar) vibrations.

So if you are surrounded by people who are holding a low vibration, you may find your own vibration is not as high as it could be. If this is the case, you may want to adjust who you surround yourself with, and surround yourself with people who will help to raise your vibration. Low vibrations can work in the same way as having a cold, you can pass it around to each other. Imagine how hard it would be to stay well and healthy if you were constantly surrounded by people who are sick or have colds every day. The more sick people you surround yourself with, the harder it is to stay healthy. It's the same thing with vibrations. The more negative people or people of low vibration you surround yourself with, the harder it is to stay spiritually healthy. However, the opposite is also true. When very healthy people, people who like to thrive and stay well, surround you, you feel uplifted. You will naturally gravitate towards encouraging each other to live a healthy lifestyle, whether it be through conversation or by example. In that environment it is hard not to stay healthy! Personally, I feel that it's important to always have people in your life helping you achieve your highest vibration possible.

This may result in you having to make some major adjustments to limit the effect some people have on your life right now. Follow the tips above, and if all else fails, you may have to resort to number eight.

8) Let unhealthy relationships go.

If all else fails, yes ... you may have to let some relationships go. If they're unhealthy and causing you discomfort, it can be a problem, which you can ignore for awhile, until it's too late. When problem relationships are allowed to be in your life for too long, the stress of these relationships will often manifest itself physically in your life and your physical body will suffer as a result. Things such as high blood pressure, heart issues, and low immune system can all be a result from dealing with the stress that comes with these toxic relationships.

People change over the years, and sometimes you're no longer a vibrational match with the people who have been in your life for years. When this becomes very apparent to you, and you've tried all of the other things here with no avail, the last resort may be to let those relationships go. Especially if the effect they're having on your life is affecting you in a very negative way. As sad as this is, it may be a spouse, mother, father, sister, brother, best friend, or boss. It doesn't have to be permanent, and you may not even want to make that determination right now, as they may change in the future, allowing the relationship to be resumed. I suggest this as a last resort, but sometimes this is the only way to minimize the affect "energy vampires" have on your life.

CHAPTER 10

ENERGY VAMPIRE FIRST AID!

So what if, despite all of the things you learned here, you were bitten? It happens to everybody, so it's helpful to know what to do. The best thing you can do is to ground yourself. There are many things you should know about grounding, and many ways you can ground yourself quickly.

So what is grounding?

Grounding is ridding yourself of excess psychic energy, which your spiritual body has picked up externally, and replenishing your physical body with energy from the earth, which is more of a physical based energy.

It is essentially bringing your spiritual and physical bodies back into balance with one another by balancing both energies.

Spiritual grounding is essentially the same as electrical grounding. When working with electricity, they long ago discovered there needed to be a place for excess electricity to go in case of a build up. Connections to the ground limit the build up of static electricity. The ground will absorb this excess electricity safely, and therefore, eliminate the possibility of major problems, such as a power outage or combustion resulting in fire. Electrical grounding also completes a circuit when needed, eliminating the need for a return conductor.

As energetic beings we operate in the same manner. We need a place for excess energy to go in case of a build up. Also, we need a return conductor when we've depleted ourselves of energy. The ground, when operating as a return conductor, will also reenergize our system.

Grounding is incredibly important. People should understand what it is and why they need to do it, otherwise it's easily bushed off as unimportant. The simple fact of the matter is you can feel so much better if you do it routinely.

How can you tell if you need to be grounded? You'll feel like you have too much excess stuff or energy attached to you, or you will feel depleted of energy.

Common Symptoms of Being Ungrounded:

- Shaky feeling or weak feeling
- Achy body or joints
- Having a hard time focusing
- Feel like you have low blood sugar (when full)
- Lethargic or unusually tired
- Dizziness
- You no longer feel "present"
- You feel spaced out or "out of body"

This is what happens when your physical energies and spiritual energies are no longer in balance.

What Causes A Spiritual/Physical Imbalance:

1) Energy vampires, or negative people.

I think this is pretty self-explanatory at this point. When you're around these types of people, you need to protect yourself energetically or they will drain energy from you for their benefit. Either way, it causes imbalance.

2) Doing too much spiritual work.

Healers, psychics or even people just discovering their own gifts and abilities are very prone to imbalance. Even going on a new spiritual journey can cause a change in balance. People tend to get so excited about the spiritual realm and what they're learning and doing that their physical bodies can begin to suffer if ignored which leads us to number three.

3) Ignoring your physical body and its needs.

When people discover their spiritual bodies, many times the physical body then gets ignored, like it's old news, or no longer important. They labor under the impression that the spiritual body always dictates physical health. While this is true in many regards, the physical body still needs things like food and exercise. The thing is you can't ignore one body or the other—they work together as a team. Many psychics and healers I know have actually had poor health, and this is why.

4) Life.

That's right, life! It just happens as you are around many people every day, doing many different things. You can't always be aware of who you are around and when, it's impossible. I do this for a living and even I'm not aware of my spiritual body 24-7 and I don't want to be. I also want to enjoy life from a physical perspective, as this is our only physical experience! So it just happens sometimes, when we aren't paying attention.

Why Should You Ground Yourself?

1) To feel better!

When you are properly grounded, you feel good! You feel spiritually good, and you feel physically good. You feel right and whole, and you feel balanced. All is right in the world when your two bodies are in alignment.

2) To strengthen your energy.

This is one of the best ways to strengthen your energy. Think of your energy and your spiritual body as having muscles, just like your physical body. Grounding is a way to flex your spiritual muscles and keep them active. They're not going to be as strong or as useful to you otherwise. Just as you need to move your physical body each day or your muscles will become weak, the same thing goes for your spiritual body. So flex those spiritual muscles!

*Helpful tip: Make grounding a routine for yourself!

I meditate before I go places, especially if I know it's going to be a heightened energy situation. I make sure to drink plenty of water (not easy for me), and I take a hot shower (with scented shower gel) at the end of the day. Lastly, I burn incense often, as it immediately shifts my energy. I have a routine for myself, and it works really well. If you don't make it a routine, it becomes a chore or hard to remember.

CHAPTER 11

SIMPLE GROUNDING TECHNIQUES

*T*here are many different ways you can ground yourself which can be confusing when you are wondering which technique to use. However, I like to use several techniques. In my opinion a combination always works best so you can integrate these techniques into more of a lifestyle routine. That way it becomes less overwhelming, and even more effective. So here are some popular grounding techniques.

1) Meditation.

Meditation is a very easy way to ground yourself. If you don't know what kind of mediation works for grounding, *any kind!* Just do it, even if it's only for a couple of minutes. If you would like to use a special grounding meditation, I have included one at the end of this chapter.

2) Through scent.

Burning incense or sage is one of the most common ways

to ground yourself through scent. I, for one, don't like the smell of sage, and the smoke can be overbearing. For everyday use, I use incense. Sandlewood is one of the most popular and effective grounding incenses to use. However, other scents work too, such as scented soaps in the shower, or perfumes, oils, and even lotions. Scents with earthy smells such as woods are the best. Remember, grounding is connecting yourself with the earth's energy, so think earthy when you are picking out scents.

3) Water.

Drinking water, swimming in water, or showering, anything that involves water is grounding. Make sure you're drinking water daily. But when you need to feel more grounded, go for a swim, sit in a hot tub, or take a shower. Water is an energy cleanser and it's one of the earth's elements, very important when grounding.

4) Exercise.

Exercise is *really important* when you're trying to keep your spiritual body and your physical body in balance and working in harmony, or when you're trying to ground yourself. This is like P90X for your spiritual body, it's spiritual grounding at its best! It also helps keep you connected with your physical body. Spiritual and physical balance is one of the biggest benefits of exercising.

5) Nature.

Go outside. Walk around. Get away from electronic devices! All of your electronic devices give off energy; the television, cell phones, computers, anything that you can plug in. So when you're indoors too much you are sponging up the wrong kind of energy. You need Earth energy to stay in balance and stay grounded. When you go outdoors and come into contact with Mother Earth, it allows any excess energy to be transferred into the ground. This could be through things such as walking, hiking, biking, sledding, skiing, wake boarding, or camping. You will also naturally draw upon the energy of Mother Earth when you're outdoors and you replace any energy that you have lost with Earth energy.

6) Yoga.

Yoga is specifically designed to align your spiritual and physical bodies! Take a class or do your own yoga poses in your living room.

7) Chocolate.

Who knew chocolate could be so good for you? However, chocolate has strong grounding properties. So eat some chocolate when you feel the need to be grounded. Dark chocolate is the best (not my favorite), but any chocolate will work. You only need a small portion, so mini candy bars are perfect.

8) Sex

Sex gets you in tune with your psychical senses and physical body very fast, therefore it is very grounding. It really heightens your physical senses and allows you to become very aware of your physical body. It also allows you to tap into each other on a spiritual level, creating balance.

. . .

WE NEED a way to rid ourselves of excess energy, we also need a way to complete a circuit and recharge ourselves when needed. Grounding does both of these things. It's all about balance. Balancing our spiritual self with our physical self. Tapping into the spiritual world and learning how to work with Mother Earth's energy, which we so desperately need on a physical level. Mother Earth's energy is very powerful, and it's important in helping us keep peace, balance, and harmony within our system.

CHAPTER 12

GROUNDING YOURSELF WITH STONES

*M*any people like to use stones to help with grounding, as some stones have natural grounding properties. I like to keep them in my pocket when I'm doing events. However, I strongly suggest if you want to use stones for grounding, wear them as jewelry. They are just as effective and the stones are way easier to keep track of. (Otherwise you may find them in the washer!)

Another good thing to do with stones is to place them near your bed or wherever you work. I do that as well. You can also place them around your house if you wish. But near where you spend a lot of time is most effective.

Five Popular Grounding Stones:

1) Iron Pyrite – Also known as fool's gold. *Iron Pyrite is an excellent stone for grounding excess energy.* Iron Pyrite is usually considered a 'solar' stone, in tune with the energy of the Sun God and helpful for channeling healing, confidence and success into your life. Mostly from Mexico or Peru, it is one of my favorites.

2) Tourmaline – *Black Tourmaline is known as a psychic protection stone.* It gives psychic protection against negative energy and psychic attack. It also brings good luck, happiness and healing.

3) Hematite – *Hematite is the all-purpose grounding (energy balancing) stone.* It is also known for stimulating the mind and enhancing memory. Hematite rings and bracelets are very common.

4) Smoky Quartz - This is a very high vibration stone. *Smoky quartz is an excellent stone for removing negativity and negative energy of any kind and transforming them to positive energy.* It is also a very protective and grounding stone.

5) Obsidian – Volcanic glass, cooled down to become a natural brown/black. Black *Obsidian* is *grounding and centering.* It represents strength. It is also a powerful cleanser of psychic smog, and is a strong psychic protection stone.

*Note: I like to wear grounding stones, in fact, that's the only jewelry that I wear. I was asked about grounding stones over the years so much that I finally just opened up a little gemstone store called Moon Child. If you're having a hard time finding gemstone jewelry, feel free to stop by. :)

https://moonchildshop.com/

CHAPTER 13

GROUNDING MEDITATION EXERCISE

*T*his meditation exercise is designed to specifically help ground yourself. It's a very effective exercise, which should be done at least once a day. It's especially helpful when you're stressed out, around a bunch of people, or have been exposed to negative energy of any kind.

1) Find a quiet place where you will not be disturbed.

2) Sit comfortably in a chair or in an upright position. Hands to your side and feet flat on the floor, don't cross your hands, feet or legs.

3) Close your eyes and concentrate on your breathing. Slow your breathing to a relaxed state.

4) When your breathing is rhythmic, concentrate on relaxing all of the muscles in your body.

5) Imagine your spine is like a string on a musical instrument. Imagine this string or cord attaches all of your chakras together, from your root chakra (base of your spine) to your crown chakra (top of your head).

6) Visualize this string or cord vibrating. Imagine you are in control of how fast or slow the vibration is. Next raise this vibration to the highest level of vibration you can achieve.

7) When you are vibrating at a high level, imagine that a red beam of light comes from above your body through the top of your head, down your spine. Feel it travel slowly through each of your chakras. Then imagine that the red beam continues out through the bottom of your tailbone, through the chair, into the earth. See the light go deep, deep into the earth until it reaches the middle. When it reaches the center of the earth, imagine anchoring the red beam to the earth.

8) Next, visualize all of the extra energy you've picked up from places you've been and the people you've seen throughout the day. See this energy naturally flowing down this light into the earth, almost as if you had rolled in dirt and you are now taking a shower. Feel the energy flow down the drain (the red beam of light), feel how clean your energetic being is becoming as this extra energy (that does not belong to you) is released into the earth.

9) See and feel this energy becoming absorbed back into the earth. Let the natural flow continue until you feel completely clean, and free of any energetic residue. Take a moment to bask in the clean feeling of your energetic being, enjoy how that feels.

10) Next, imagine a white light coming from the middle of Mother Earth, coming up through the ground, to your chair, gently coming up through your root chakra, continuing to touch each chakra as it travels to the top of your head. This white light is recharging your energetic field with new energy from Mother Earth, replacing any of your own energy that you have lost throughout the day. Feel this energy recharging your system as it fills each chakra and continues up the spine and out through the top of your head.

11) Each time this new energy moves through a chakra, imagine that it disperses energy to other parts of the body.

Feel the energy disperse, kind of like when you watch fireworks explode. You can do this as long as you like.

12) Remain in this state until you feel a sense of completion, then release this image into the Universe.

I like to do this every morning, although many people enjoy doing this exercise at night. There is no right or wrong amount of time you spend, you should adjust the time to whatever feels right to you.

*NOTE: I've created a Grounding Meditation here for those who find it easier to have one in audio. https://keystothespiritworld.com/product/grounding-meditation

ABOUT THE AUTHOR

Aloha! My name is Jennifer O'Neill and I am an Empath specialist...

I was born looking at the world differently than most everyone else around me. The funny thing is I thought everyone was like me.

It wasn't until I got older that I realized...I was born with a very special connection to the spirit world.

This connection has allowed me to access things you can benefit from. Lots of information on how things work in the spiritual realm, how things work energetically in the physical realm, as well as how this information can help you to enhance your life and help you to live the best life possible.

I was born a very strong Empath. I was gifted with this ability with a purpose, to teach others. To show you that you have some of these same abilities, and to simplify the process of using these spiritual tools and gifts you were born with in a way that fits into your everyday life.

Mahalo,

Jennifer

Jennifer is the author of several books and is also the creator and founder of Empath University. She is also one of Hawaii's top psychics and a leading expert in the field of spirit communication. She has spent the last twenty years as a professional psychic and spiritual teacher helping people all over the world learn how to develop themselves spiritually.

★ CONTINUE YOUR SPIRITUAL JOURNEY BELOW ★

Keys To The Spirit World >>>

www.keystothespiritworld.com >>>

★ FREE MEDITATIONS ★
(links at keystothespiritworld.com)

★ THE EMPOWERED EMPATH PODCAST ★
(links at keystothespiritworld.com)

YouTube
Spotify
iTunes

★ EMPATH UNIVERSITY CLASSES ★

(link https://empath-university.com/)

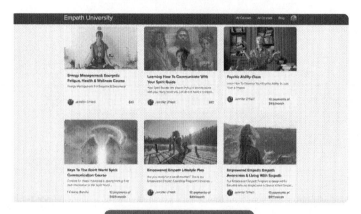

★ CONNECT WITH ME ★

instagram.com/keystothespiritworld

pinterest.com/keystothespirit

twitter.com/keystothespirit